moda
BAKE SHOP

Rollin' Along

Quick and Easy Quilts from 2½" Strips

Compiled by Lissa Alexander

Martingale®
Create with Confidence

Moda Bake Shop
Rollin' Along: Quick and Easy Quilts from 2½" Strips
© 2022 by Martingale & Company®

Martingale®
18939 120th Ave. NE, Ste. 101
Bothell, WA 98011-9511 USA
ShopMartingale.com

Printed in Hong Kong
27 26 25 24 23 22   8 7 6 5 4 3 2 1

Library of Congress Cataloging-in-Publication Data is available upon request.

ISBN: 978-1-68356-182-8

MISSION STATEMENT

We empower makers who use fabric and yarn to make life more enjoyable.

CREDITS

PUBLISHER AND
CHIEF VISIONARY OFFICER
Jennifer Erbe Keltner

CONTENT DIRECTOR
Karen Costello Soltys

TECHNICAL EDITOR
Elizabeth Tisinger Beese

COPY EDITOR
Durby Peterson

ILLUSTRATOR
Lisa Lauch

DESIGN MANAGER
Adrienne Smitke

PRODUCTION MANAGER
Regina Girard

COVER AND
BOOK DESIGNER
Mia Mar

PHOTOGRAPHERS
Brent Kane
Adam Albright

Contents

Welcome to the Moda Bake Shop!

Thank you for stopping by the Moda Bake Shop, the place where up-and-coming quilt designers gather to share recipes for their latest quilt patterns.

We asked a dozen designers for a Jelly Roll–friendly pattern, and the result is *Rollin' Along*! We know that quilters love to buy these rolled-up bundles of 2½"-wide fabric strips. In each Jelly Roll, you get 40 strips: at least one of every fabric in a collection. (That's just about 3 yards total, enough fabrics to make a beautifully coordinated scrap quilt.) These rolls are fun to collect, easy to display, and they provide enough fabric to get you on your way toward a generously sized lap quilt or even a bed-size quilt.

We also know that quilters are often tempted to buy these treats without a specific pattern in mind. But that shouldn't mean your collection goes unused! Now you have in your hands a book filled with 12 brand-new designs created especially for using these tempting precuts.

Whether or not you have the specific fabric line shown in the pictured quilts, you're bound to find a pattern you love that's perfect for a Jelly Roll you already own. Or, go ahead and visit your local quilt shop for a brand-new Jelly Roll or two so you can re-create the quilts shown. Either way, you'll be on your way to a quick finish, since all the 2½" strips are already cut for you. It's just one more thing to love about Jelly Rolls: they let you get to the fun part faster!

Lissa Alexander

Rose Compass

Whether you're heading north, south, east, or west, Rose Compass will add joy to your journey. Rich with color, each block is a beauty. And like a compass to guide you, Melissa's instructions make it so easy to create this gorgeous design.

Finished quilt: 90½" × 90½" ✳ Finished blocks: 20" × 20"

Materials

Yardage is based on 42"-wide fabric and two identical Jelly Rolls (precut 2½" strips). A Moda Fabrics Jelly Roll contains 40 strips. Melissa used the Dance in Paris collection by Zen Chic for Moda Fabrics.

- 80 strips, 2½" × 42" *each*, of assorted pink, blue, green, and gray prints for blocks, sashing, and binding
- 5¾ yards of white print for block backgrounds and sashing
- 8¼ yards of fabric for backing
- 99" × 99" piece of batting

Cutting

All measurements include ¼"-wide seam allowances. Sort the 80 print 2½"-wide strips into five groups of 16 strips each. Groups 4 and 5 need to be identical, with the same 16 prints in each group.

From *each* of the strips in group 1, cut:

12 squares, 2½" × 2½" (192 total; label as A)

From *each* of the strips in group 2, cut:

12 squares, 2½" × 2½" (192 total; label as B)

From *each* of the strips in group 3, cut:

2 pieces, 2½" × 8½" (32 total; label as E)

2 pieces, 2½" × 4½" (32 total; label as D)

4 squares, 2½" × 2½" (64 total; label as C)

From *each* of the strips in group 4, cut:

3 strips, 2½" × 12½" (48 total; label as F)

From *each* of the strips in group 5, cut:

1 strip, 2½" × 26" (16 total; label as binding)

1 strip, 2½" × 12½" (16 total; label as F)

From the remaining scraps of 2½"-wide strips, cut a *total* of:

25 squares, 2½" × 2½" (label as sashing)

From the white print, cut:

12 strips, 6½" × 42"; crosscut into 192 strips, 2½" × 6½"

13 strips, 4½" × 42"; crosscut into:
- 80 squares, 4½" × 4½"
- 64 pieces, 2½" × 4½"

20 strips, 2½" × 42"; crosscut into 40 strips, 2½" × 20½"

Making the Blocks

For each block you'll use four different prints: one print for the A squares; a second print for the B squares; a third print for the C, D, and E pieces; and a fourth print for the F strips. Press seam allowances in the directions indicated by the arrows.

1. For one block, gather:
- 12 A squares
- 12 B squares
- 4 C squares
- 2 D pieces
- 2 E pieces
- 4 F strips

Draw a diagonal line from corner to corner on the wrong side of the A, B, and C squares.

2. Position a marked A square on each end of an E piece with right sides together, aligning raw edges as shown. Sew on the marked lines and then trim ¼" from the sewn lines to make a unit measuring 2½" × 8½", including seam allowances. Make two units.

Make 2 units,
2½" × 8½".

3. Sew D pieces to opposite edges of a white 4½" square. Add units from step 2 to the top and bottom edges to make a center unit measuring 8½" square, including seam allowances.

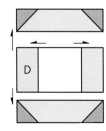

Make 1 center unit,
8½" × 8½".

4. Position a marked B square on the right end of a white 2½" × 4½" piece with right sides together. Sew on the marked line and then trim ¼" from the sewn line. Make two units and two mirror-image units as shown, pressing the seam allowances in opposite directions.

Make 2 of each unit,
2½" × 4½".

5. Join one of each unit in step 4 to make a unit measuring 2½" × 8½", including seam allowances. Make two units.

Make 2 units,
2½" × 8½".

6. Position a marked B square on the right end of a white 2½" × 6½" strip with right sides together. Sew on the marked line and then trim ¼" from the sewn line. Make two units and two mirror-image units as shown, pressing the seam allowances in opposite directions.

Make 2 of each unit,
2½" × 6½".

7. Join one of each unit in step 6 as shown to make a unit measuring 2½" × 12½", including seam allowances. Make two units.

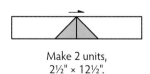

Make 2 units,
2½" × 12½".

Designed, pieced, and quilted by Melissa Corry

See more of Melissa's patterns at HappyQuiltingMelissa.com.

press as shown. Make four corner units measuring 4½" square, including seam allowances.

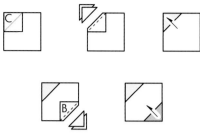

Make 4 corner units,
4½" × 4½".

10. Using marked A squares instead of B squares, refer to step 6 to make four units and four mirror-image units. Join these units as in step 7 to make four units. Sew an F strip to the bottom of each unit to make four side units.

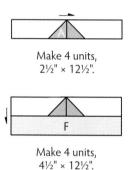

Make 4 units,
2½" × 12½".

Make 4 units,
4½" × 12½".

8. Sew step 5 units to opposite edges of the center unit. Add step 7 units to the remaining edges. The center unit should now be 12½" square, including seam allowances.

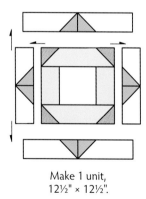

Make 1 unit,
12½" × 12½".

9. Align a marked C square with one corner of a white 4½" square. Sew on the marked line and then trim ¼" from the sewn line. Repeat to add a marked B square to the opposite corner; be sure to

11. Lay out four corner units from step 9, four side units from step 10, and one center unit from step 8 in three rows. Sew together the pieces in each row, then join the rows to make a block measuring 20½" square, including seam allowances. Repeat to make 16 blocks.

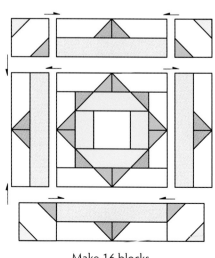

Make 16 blocks,
20½" × 20½".

Assembling the Quilt Top

1. Lay out the pieced blocks in four rows of four blocks each, placing white 2½" × 20½" sashing strips between the blocks and along the outer edges of the blocks. Sew together the pieces in each row to make four rows, 20½" × 90½".

2. Lay out four white strips and five assorted 2½" sashing squares in a row. Sew the pieces together to make a sashing row measuring 2½" × 90½", including seam allowances. Make five rows.

3. Alternating sashing rows and block rows, join the rows to make a quilt top that measures 90½" square.

Finishing the Quilt

For more details on any finishing steps, visit ShopMartingale.com/HowtoQuilt for free downloadable information.

1. Prepare the quilt backing so it's about 8" larger in both directions than the quilt top.

2. Layer the quilt top with batting and backing; baste the layers together.

3. Quilt by hand or machine. The quilt shown is machine quilted with an allover pattern of large and small loops.

4. Use the assorted print 2½" × 26" strips from group 5 to make double-fold binding. Attach the binding to the quilt.

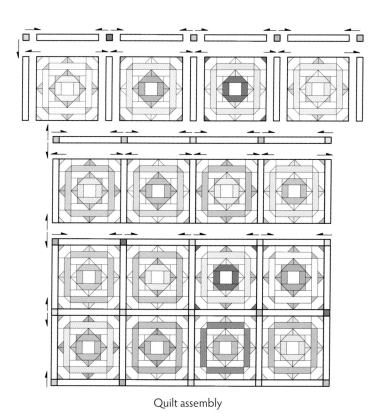

Quilt assembly

Garden Lattice

It pays to look up! Susan used a Jelly Roll to create a quilted version of a garden setting she admired on a recent trip to a botanical garden. The lattice had a cascading mix of flowers tumbling out of it, and Susan captured the lovely feel of that scene through the mix of colors in her fabric choices.

Finished quilt: 65½" × 81¾" ✳ **Finished blocks: 10" × 10"**

Materials

Yardage is based on 42"-wide fabric and one Jelly Roll (precut 2½" strips). Susan used the Songbook collection by Fancy That Design House for Moda Fabrics. A Moda Fabrics Jelly Roll contains 40 strips.

- 32 strips, 2½" × 42" *each*, of assorted prints for blocks
- 2⅔ yards of cream print for block backgrounds and sashing
- ¼ yard of steel blue print for sashing squares
- 1½ yards of teal print for setting and corner triangles
- ⅝ yard of navy print for binding
- 5 yards of fabric for backing
- 72" × 88" piece of batting

Cutting

All measurements include ¼"-wide seam allowances.

From *each* of the assorted print 2½"-wide strips, cut:
4 pieces, 2½" × 6½" (128 total)
4 squares, 2½" × 2½" (128 total)

From the cream print, cut:
4 strips, 10½" × 42"; crosscut into 80 strips, 2" × 10½"
18 strips, 2½" × 42"; crosscut into 288 squares, 2½" × 2½"

From the steel blue print, cut:
3 strips, 2" × 42"; crosscut into 49 squares, 2" × 2"

From the navy print, cut:
8 strips, 2½" × 42"

From the teal print, cut:
2 strips, 18" × 42"; crosscut into 4 squares, 18" × 18". Cut the squares into quarters diagonally to yield 16 setting triangles (2 will be extra).
1 strip, 10" × 42"; crosscut into 2 squares, 10" × 10". Cut the squares in half diagonally to yield 4 corner triangles. (If you're using a directional print as in the featured quilt, cut one square from upper left to lower right and the other square from lower left to upper right, as shown below.)

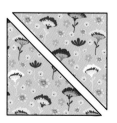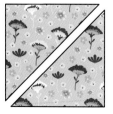

Cut corner setting triangles in opposite directions.

2. Lay out the four print squares and five cream 2½" squares in three rows as shown. Sew together the pieces in each row. Join the rows to make a nine-patch unit measuring 6½" square, including seam allowances.

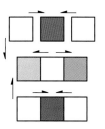

Make a nine-patch unit,
6½" × 6½".

3. Lay out the four print 2½" × 6½" pieces, four cream print 2½" squares, and the nine-patch unit from step 2 in three rows as shown. Sew together the pieces in each row. Join the rows to make a block, which should be 10½" square, including seam allowances. Repeat steps 1–3 to make 32 blocks total.

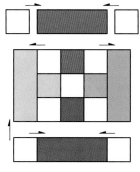

Make 32 blocks,
10½" × 10½".

Cutting Setting Triangles

Jelly Rolls are an economical way to have a piece of every fabric in a collection. However, due to the way the fabrics are precut, you don't have flexibility for orienting directional prints, which can create a scattered look in your quilt. Cutting and arranging the setting triangles in the final assembly as shown on page 12 will help create an overall direction for your quilt and tie your project together.

Making the Blocks

Press seam allowances in the directions indicated by the arrows.

1. For one block, gather a 2½" × 6½" piece and a matching 2½" square from four different prints.

Assembling the Quilt Top

1. Referring to the quilt assembly diagram on page 16, lay out the blocks, cream sashing strips, steel blue sashing squares, and teal corner and oversized setting triangles in diagonal rows. Sew together the pieces in each row. Join each block row to its sashing row *before* adding the side triangles. On block row 5 (the longest row), you need to add a sashing row to both the top and bottom of the block row before you can add the setting triangles. Join the rows and add the corner triangles to make the quilt center.

Designed and pieced by Susan Vaughan; quilted by Marion Bott

Follow Susan's sewing adventures on Instgram @thefeltedpear.

2. Trim the quilt ¼" past the centers of the steel blue sashing squares. The quilt should measure 65½" × 81¾".

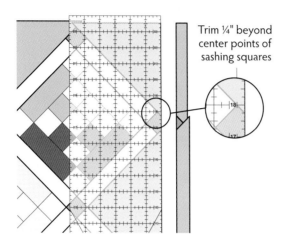

Trim ¼" beyond center points of sashing squares

Finishing the Quilt

For more details on any finishing steps, visit ShopMartingale.com/HowtoQuilt for free downloadable information.

1. Prepare the quilt backing so it's about 6" larger in both directions than the quilt top.

2. Layer the quilt top with batting and backing; baste the layers together.

3. Quilt by hand or machine. The quilt shown is machine quilted with an allover Baptist Fan design.

4. Use the navy 2½"-wide strips to make double-fold binding. Attach the binding to the quilt.

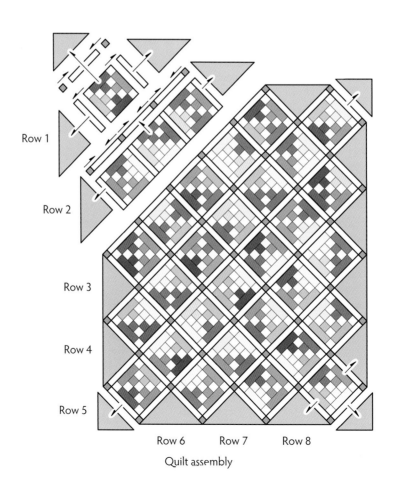

Row 1

Row 2

Row 3

Row 4

Row 5

Row 6   Row 7   Row 8

Quilt assembly

Family Picnic

Corinne proclaims that she loves strip piecing and all the fun things you can do with fabric when you cut your strip sets in a variety of ways. This quilt is perfect for picnic time and can be made by coordinating your colors or mixing things up and going completely random and scrappy!

Finished quilt: 82½" × 99½" ✳ **Finished blocks: 8" × 8"**

Materials

Yardage is based on 42"-wide fabric and two Jelly Rolls (precut 2½" strips). The Jelly Rolls don't have to be the same, but it's probably easiest to get the necessary matching pairs of beige prints if you start with two matching Jelly Rolls. A Moda Fabrics Jelly Roll contains 40 strips. Corinne used the Make Time Collection by Aneela Hoey for Moda Fabrics. Divide your Jelly Rolls into like colors as noted below.

- 12 strips, 2½" × 42" *each*, of assorted blue prints for blocks
- 7 strips, 2½" × 42" *each*, of assorted light blue prints for blocks
- 8 strips, 2½" × 42" *each*, of assorted pink prints for blocks
- 11 strips, 2½" × 42" *each*, of assorted red prints for blocks
- 10 strips, 2½" × 42" *each*, of assorted light red prints for blocks
- 24 strips, 2½" × 42" *each*, of assorted beige prints for sashing (6 pairs of identical prints, plus 12 more strips)
- 5 yards of white solid for blocks and sashing
- ¾ yard of red plaid for binding
- 9¾ yards of fabric for backing
- 91" × 108" piece of batting

Cutting

All measurements include ¼"-wide seam allowances.

From the white solid, cut:

20 strips, 2½" × 42"; crosscut 16 of the strips into 63 strips, 2½" × 8½"

74 strips, 1½" × 42"; crosscut 6 of the strips into:
- 24 strips, 1½" × 8½"
- 6 pieces, 1½" × 3"

From the red plaid, cut:

10 strips, 2½" x 42"

Strip Piecing

When strip piecing be sure to alternate the direction you sew the strips of fabric together to prevent warping to one side. Starch is your friend. Spray each strip and press until dry *before* sewing the strip sets.

Making the Blocks

Press seam allowances in the directions indicated by the arrows.

1. Sort the blue, light blue, pink, red, and light red 2½" × 42" strips into sets of three to make the following sets from each color. (The leftover strips will be used in step 4.)

- 3 sets of blue
- 2 sets of light blue
- 2 sets of pink
- 3 sets of red
- 2 sets of light red

2. Alternating colors, sew together one set from step 1 with two white 1½" × 42" strips to make strip set A. Make 12 of strip set A.

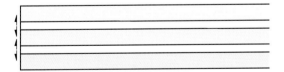

Make 12 A strip sets, 8½" × 42".

3. Cut each strip set into four A blocks, 8½" square including seam allowances. Cut 48 blocks.

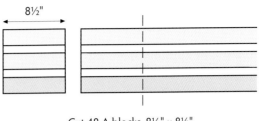

Cut 48 A blocks, 8½" × 8½"
(4 from each strip set).

Extra Variety

You will only need 44 A blocks in the finished quilt. Instructions are given for making 48 blocks to give you more fabric variety, plus added flexibility when laying out the quilt and distributing colors.

4. Alternating colors, sew together three remaining assorted print strips and two white 1½" × 42" strips to make strip set B. Make four of strip set B.

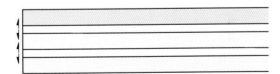

Make 4 B strip sets, 8½" × 42".

5. Cut each strip set into nine B segments, 2½" × 8½" including seam allowances. Cut 36 segments.

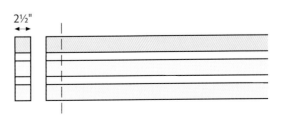

Cut 36 B segments, 2½" × 8½"
(9 from each strip set).

6. Lay out three assorted (not matching) B segments and two white 1½" × 8½" strips as shown. Sew together the pieces to make a B block, which should be 8½" square, including seam allowances. Make 12 B blocks.

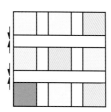

Make 12 B blocks,
8½" × 8½".

Making the Sashing Units

1. Sew together two matching beige strips end to end. Trim the strip to 82½" long. Repeat with remaining pairs of matching beige strips to make six beige sashing strips total.

2. Sew together two white 1½" × 42" strips end to end. Trim the strip to 82½". Repeat to make 12 skinny white sashing strips total.

3. Sew together two white 2½" × 42" strips end to end. Trim the strip to 82½". Repeat to make two wide white sashing strips.

4. Alternating colors, sew together six remaining beige strips and six remaining white 1½" × 42" strips to make strip set C.

Make 1 C strip set, 18½" × 42".

Pressing the Sashing

When making the sashing strips in steps 1 through 3 at left, press the sashing seam allowances open, or pay attention to which direction you press them so that the beige strips nest together with the white strips where applicable.

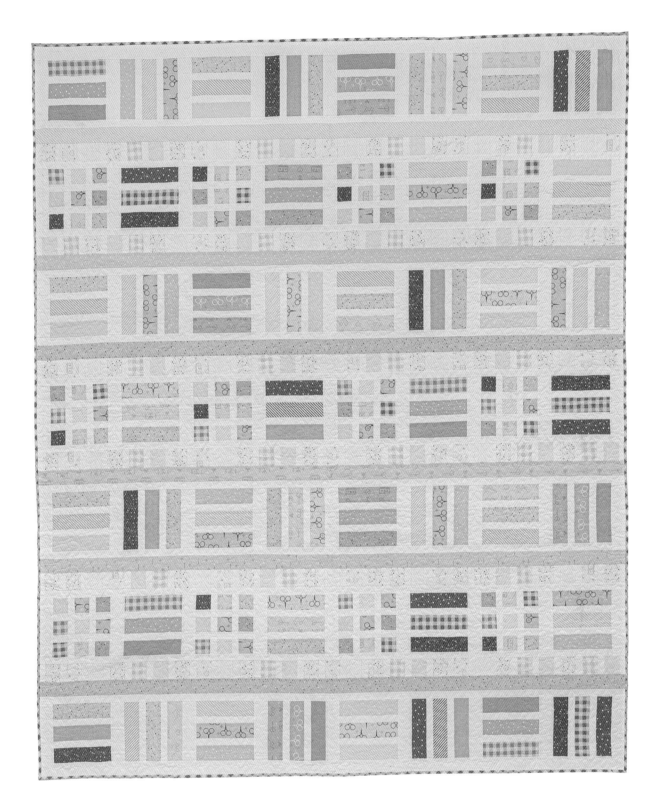

Designed and pieced by Corinne Sovey; quilted by Sarah Campbell of Stitch Mode Quilts

See more from Corinne on Instagram @corrine.sovey or at CorinneSovey.com.

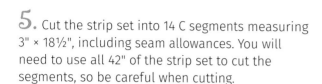

5. Cut the strip set into 14 C segments measuring 3" × 18½", including seam allowances. You will need to use all 42" of the strip set to cut the segments, so be careful when cutting.

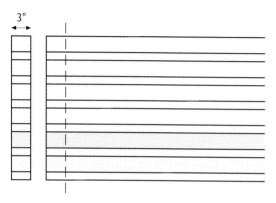

Cut 14 C segments, 3" × 18½".

6. Cut the remaining six beige strips into six 2½" × 32" strips and six 2½" × 10" strips. Cut six remaining white 1½" × 42" strips into six 1½" × 32" strips and six 1½" × 10" strips.

7. Alternating colors, sew together the six beige 2½" × 32" strips and six white 1½" × 32" strips to make a short strip set C. Cut the strip set into 10 C segments measuring 3" × 18½", including seam allowances.

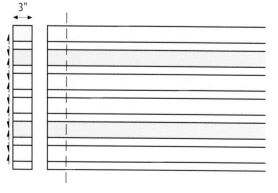

Make a second C strip set, 18½" × 32".
Cut 10 C segments, 3" × 18½".

8. Alternating colors, sew together three beige 2½" × 10" strips and three white 1½" × 10" strips to make a strip set D. Make two strip sets. Cut each strip set into three D segments measuring 3" × 9½", including seam allowances.

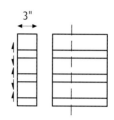

Make 2 D strip sets, 9½" × 10".
Cut 6 D segments, 3" × 9½"
(3 from each strip set).

Assembling the Quilt Top

1. Lay out nine white 2½" × 8½" strips and eight A blocks in a row, alternating blocks and strips and rotating every other block 90°. Sew together the pieces to make a block A row measuring 8½" × 82½", including seam allowances. Make four block A rows.

Make 4 rows, 8½" × 82½".

2. Lay out nine white 2½" × 8½" pieces, four B blocks, and four A blocks in a row, alternating the blocks and strips. Sew together the pieces to make an A/B block row. The row should be 8½" × 82½", including seam allowances. Make three A/B block rows. You will have four A blocks left over.

Make 3 rows, 8½" × 82½".

3. Sew together four C segments, one D segment, and one white 1½" × 3" piece to make a pieced sashing row. The row should be 3" × 82½", including seam allowances. Make six pieced sashing rows.

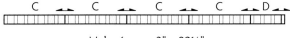

Make 6 rows, 3" × 82½".

4. Referring to the quilt assembly diagram below, lay out the wide white sashing strips, block rows, skinny white sashing strips, beige sashing strips, and pieced sashing strips. Join the rows to complete the quilt top, which should be 82½" × 99½".

Finishing the Quilt

For more details on any finishing steps, visit ShopMartingale.com/HowtoQuilt for free downloadable information.

1. Prepare the quilt backing so it's about 8" larger in both directions than the quilt top.

2. Layer the quilt top with batting and backing; baste the layers together.

3. Quilt by hand or machine. The quilt shown is machine quilted with an allover flower pattern.

4. Use the red plaid 2½"-wide strips to make double-fold binding. Attach the binding to the quilt.

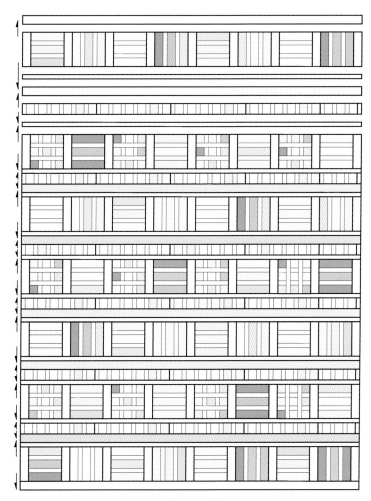

Quilt assembly

Summertime Fun

What a refreshing color palette results when you combine a classic red-white-and-blue scheme with a delightful splash of pink! In Summertime Fun, Jessica shows that unexpected color combinations can add zest to your quilt. So get out your favorite fabrics and show your colors!

Finished quilt: 75½" × 75½" ✳ **Finished blocks: 9" × 9"**

Materials

Yardage is based on 42"-wide fabric and one Jelly Roll (precut 2½" strips). A Moda Fabrics Jelly Roll contains 40 strips. Jessica used the Belle Isle collection by Minick and Simpson for Moda Fabrics.

- 37 strips, 2½" × 42" *each*, of assorted red, blue, and pink prints for blocks
- 2⅞ yards of white solid for blocks
- ⅝ yard of off-white stripe for inner border
- ⅝ yard of navy floral for middle border
- ⅝ yard of white floral for outer border
- ⅝ yard of dark red print for binding
- 4⅝ yards of fabric for backing
- 82" × 82" piece of batting

Cutting

All measurements include ¼"-wide seam allowances.

From *each* of 13 assorted print strips, cut for A blocks:

16 squares, 2½" × 2½" (208 total; 8 will be extra)

From *each* of the 24 remaining print strips, cut for B blocks*:

4 pieces, 2½" × 5½" (96 total)

8 squares, 2½" × 2½" (192 total)

From the white solid, cut:

14 strips, 5½" × 42"; crosscut into:
- 49 squares, 5½" × 5½"
- 100 pieces, 2½" × 5½"

6 strips, 2½" × 42"; crosscut into 96 squares, 2½" × 2½"

From the off-white stripe, cut:

7 strips, 2½" × 42"

From the navy floral, cut:

8 strips, 2½" × 42"

From the white floral, cut:

8 strips, 2½" × 42"

From the dark red print, cut:

8 strips, 2½" × 42"

*Cut carefully because you need the entire 42" length of each strip.

3. Lay out the four unmarked print 2½" squares, four white 2½" × 5½" pieces, and the block center in three rows. Sew together the pieces in each row. Join the rows to make block A, which should be 9½" square, including seam allowances. Repeat to make 25 A blocks.

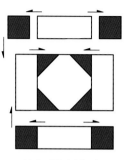

Make 25 A blocks,
9½" × 9½".

Making the B Blocks

1. For one B block, gather eight matching print 2½" squares and four of the same matching print 2½" × 5½" pieces, one white 5½" square, and four white 2½" squares. Draw a diagonal line from corner to corner on the wrong side of four print squares and the white 2½" squares.

2. Using four marked print 2½" squares and the white 5½" square, refer to step 2 of "Making the A Blocks" at left to make a block center.

Make a block center,
5½" × 5½".

3. Place a marked white square on an unmarked print 2½" square, right sides together. Sew on the drawn line. Trim the excess, ¼" beyond the stitched line. Repeat to make four half-square-triangle units, each 2½" square, including seam allowances.

Make 4 units,
2½" × 2½".

Making the A Blocks

Press seam allowances in the directions indicated by the arrows.

1. For one A block, gather eight matching print 2½" squares, one white 5½" square, and four white 2½" × 5½" pieces. Draw a diagonal line from corner to corner on the wrong side of four print squares.

2. Align a marked print square with one corner of the white 5½" square, right sides together. Sew on the drawn line. Trim the excess, ¼" beyond the stitched line. Press the resulting triangle toward the print. Add marked print squares to the remaining corners of the white square in the same manner to make a block center.

Make a block center,
5½" × 5½".

Designed and made by Jessica Dayon

Visit Jessica on Instagram @jessicadayon.

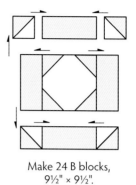

4 Lay out the four half-square-triangle units, four print 2½" × 5½" pieces, and the block center in three rows. Sew together the pieces in each row. Join the rows to make block B, which should be 9½" square, including seam allowances. Repeat to make 24 B blocks.

Make 24 B blocks,
9½" × 9½".

Assembling the Quilt Top

1. Alternating A and B blocks, lay out the blocks in seven rows of seven blocks each as shown in the quilt assembly diagram below. Sew the blocks into rows. Join the rows to complete the quilt center, which should measure 63½" square, including the seam allowances.

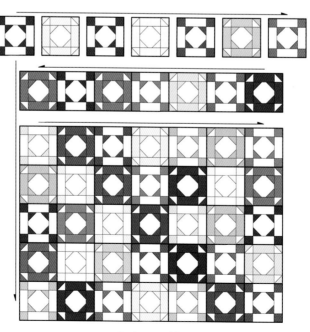

Quilt assembly

2. Join the off-white stripe 2½" × 42" strips together end to end. Trim two pieces measuring 63½" long. Sew these strips to the sides of the quilt center. Press. Trim two more strips to 67½" long. Sew these strips to the top and bottom edges.

3. Join the navy 2½" × 42" strips together end to end. Trim two pieces measuring 67½" long. Sew these strips to the sides of the quilt center. Press. Trim two more strips to 71½" long. Sew these strips to the top and bottom edges.

4. Join the white floral 2½" × 42" strips together end to end. Trim two pieces measuring 71½" long. Sew these strips to the sides of the quilt top. Press. Trim more two strips to 75½" long. Sew these strips to the top and bottom edges to complete the quilt top, which should be 75½" square, including the seam allowances.

Finishing the Quilt

For more details on any finishing steps, visit ShopMartingale.com/HowtoQuilt for free downloadable information.

1. Prepare the quilt backing so it's about 6" larger in both directions than the quilt top.

2. Layer the quilt top with batting and backing; baste the layers together.

3. Quilt by hand or machine. The quilt shown is machine quilted with an allover meander.

4. Use the dark red 2½"-wide strips to make double-fold binding. Attach the binding to the quilt.

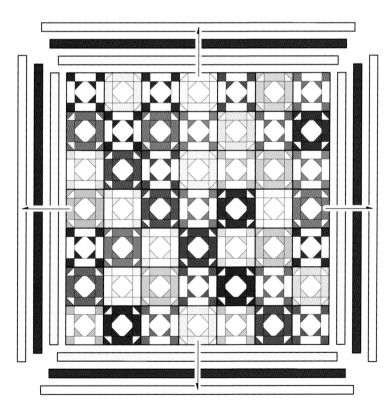

Adding borders

Backcountry Cabins

Things don't get much cozier than a cabin in the woods—especially if there's a fire roaring in the fireplace! Jen nestled her cabins and some stately pine trees in the spaces created by the traditional Irish Chain setting.

Finished quilt: 74½" × 74½" ✳ **Finished blocks: 10" × 10"**

Materials

Yardage is based on 42"-wide fabric and one Jelly Roll (precut 2½" strips). A Moda Fabrics Jelly Roll contains 40 strips. Jen used the Home Sweet Holidays collection by Deb Strain for Moda Fabrics. Divide your Jelly Roll into like colors as noted below.

- 14 strips, 2½" × 42" *each*, of assorted red prints for Irish Chain blocks and cabins in Cabin blocks
- 7 strips, 2½" × 42" *each*, of assorted black prints for Irish Chain blocks and roofs in Cabin blocks
- 5 strips, 2½" × 42" *each*, of assorted gray prints for Irish Chain blocks, doors in Cabin blocks, and tree trunks in Tree blocks
- 4 yards of cream print for background
- 8 strips, 2½" × 42" *each*, of assorted green prints for trees in Tree blocks
- ⅝ yard of black print for border
- ⅝ yard of red-and-black plaid for binding
- 4⅝ yards of fabric for backing
- 81" × 81" piece of batting
- Acrylic ruler with 45° marking

Cutting

All measurements include ¼"-wide seam allowances.

From *each* of 12 red print strips, cut:
1 piece, 2½" × 6½" (12 total)
2 pieces, 2½" × 4½" (24 total)
10 squares, 2½" × 2½" (120 total)

From *each* of the 2 remaining red print strips, cut:
15 squares, 2½" × 2½" (30 total)

From *each* of 6 black print strips, cut:
8 pieces, 2½" × 4½" (48 total)
2 squares, 2½" × 2½" (12 total)

From the remaining black print strip, cut:
15 squares, 2½" × 2½"

From *each* of 4 gray print strips, cut:
3 pieces, 2½" × 4½" (12 total)
3 pieces, 1½" × 2½" (12 total)
9 squares, 2½" × 2½" (36 total)

From the remaining gray print strip, cut:
15 squares, 2½" × 2½"

Continued on page 32

Continued from page 30

From the cream print, cut:

3 strips, 5½" × 42"; crosscut into 24 pieces,
4½" × 5½"

43 strips, 2½" × 42"; crosscut into:
- 124 pieces, 2½" × 6½"
- 24 pieces, 2½" × 5"
- 24 pieces, 2½" × 3½"
- 24 pieces, 2½" × 3"
- 220 squares, 2½" × 2½"
- 24 pieces, 2" × 2½"

From *each* of 4 green print strips, cut:

2 strips, 2½" × 7½" (8 total)

1 strip, 2½" × 6½" (4 total)

1 piece, 2½" × 5½" (4 total)

2 pieces, 2½" × 4½" (8 total)

From *each* of 4 remaining green print strips, cut:

1 strip, 2½" × 7½" (4 total)

2 strips, 2½" × 6½" (8 total)

2 pieces, 2½" × 5½" (8 total)

1 piece, 2½" × 4½" (4 total)

From the black print for border, cut:

8 strips, 2½" × 42"

From the red-and-black plaid, cut:

8 strips, 2½" × 42"

Making the Irish Chain Blocks

Press seam allowances in the directions indicated by the arrows.

1. Lay out five assorted red, black, and gray 2½" squares and four cream 2½" squares in three rows as shown. Sew together the pieces in each row. Join the rows to make a nine-patch unit measuring 6½" square, including seam allowances. Make 25 units.

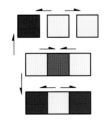

Make 25 nine-patch units,
6½" × 6½".

2. Lay out four assorted red, black, and gray 2½" squares; four cream 2½" × 6½" pieces; and a nine-patch unit in three rows as shown. Sew together the pieces in each row. Join the rows to make an Irish Chain block measuring 10½" square, including seam allowances. Make 25 blocks. (You will have three squares left over.)

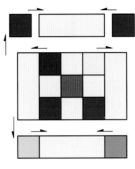

Make 25 blocks,
10½" × 10½".

Making the Tree Blocks

1. Draw a diagonal line from corner to corner on the wrong side of 96 cream 2½" squares.

2. Align a marked cream square with one end of a green 2½" × 4½" piece, right sides together. Stitch along the marked line. Trim the excess fabric ¼" from the seam. Repeat at the opposite end of the green piece, paying careful attention to the orientation of the stitching line, to make a flying-geese unit measuring 2½" × 4½", including seam allowances. Make 12 units.

Make 12 units,
2½" × 4½".

Designed, pieced, and quilted by Jen Daly

See more of Jen's designs at JenDalyQuilts.com.

3. Sew a cream 2½" × 3½" piece to each end of a flying-geese unit to make a tree unit A measuring 2½" × 10½", including seam allowances. Make 12 units.

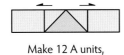

Make 12 A units,
2½" × 10½".

4. In the same manner as step 2, add a marked cream 2½" square to each end of a green 2½" × 5½" piece. Then sew a cream 2½" × 3" piece to each end of the unit to make a tree unit B measuring 2½" × 10½", including seam allowances. Make 12 units.

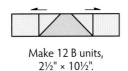

Make 12 B units,
2½" × 10½".

5. In the same manner as step 2, add a marked cream 2½" square to each end of a green 2½" × 6½" piece. Then sew a cream 2½" square to each end of the unit to make a tree unit C measuring 2½" × 10½", including seam allowances. Make 12 units.

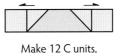

Make 12 C units,
2½" × 10½".

6. In the same manner as step 2, add a marked cream 2½" square to each end of a green 2½" × 7½" piece. Then sew a cream 2" × 2½" piece to each end of the unit to make a tree unit D measuring 2½" × 10½", including seam allowances. Make 12 units.

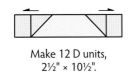

Make 12 D units,
2½" × 10½".

7. Sew a cream 2½" × 5" piece to each side of a gray 1½" × 2½" piece to make a tree trunk unit measuring 2½" × 10½", including seam allowances. Make 12 units.

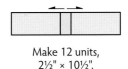

Make 12 units,
2½" × 10½".

8. Lay out one each of the tree units in a column as shown. Join the units to make a Tree block measuring 10½" square, including seam allowances. Make 12 Tree blocks.

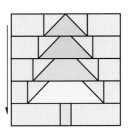

Make 12 blocks,
10½" × 10½".

Making the Cabin Blocks

1. Sew together four assorted black 2½" × 4½" pieces in a row to make unit E measuring 4½" × 8½", including seam allowances. Make 12 units.

Make 12 E units,
4½" × 8½".

2. On the wrong side of a cream 4½" × 5½" piece, start in one corner and draw a 45° line to make a right roof rectangle. Paying careful attention to the alignment of the drawn line, repeat to make a left roof rectangle. Make 12 of each.

Make 12   Make 12
left roof   right roof
rectangles.   rectangles.

3. Layer a marked right roof rectangle on the right end of an E unit with right sides together and top and right edges aligned. The bottom edge of the right roof rectangle will extend beyond the bottom edge of the E unit. Stitch along the marked line. Trim the excess fabric ¼" from the seam. In the same manner, sew a marked left roof rectangle to the left end of the E unit as shown. Trim and press as before to make a roof unit measuring 4½" × 10½", including seam allowances. Make 12 units.

 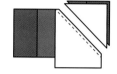

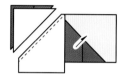 

Make 12 units,
4½" × 10½".

4. Sew together two matching red 2½" × 4½" pieces and one gray 2½" × 4½" piece. Sew a matching red print 2½" × 6½" piece to the top to make a door unit measuring 6½" square, including seam allowances. Make 12 units.

Make 12 door units,
6½" × 6½".

5. Sew cream 2½" × 6½" pieces to opposites sides of the door unit to make a cabin unit measuring 6½" × 10½", including seam allowances. Make 12 units.

Make 12 cabin units,
6½" × 10½".

6. Join a roof and cabin unit to make a Cabin block measuring 10½" square, including seam allowances. Make 12 blocks.

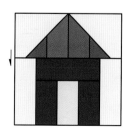

Make 12 blocks,
10½" × 10½".

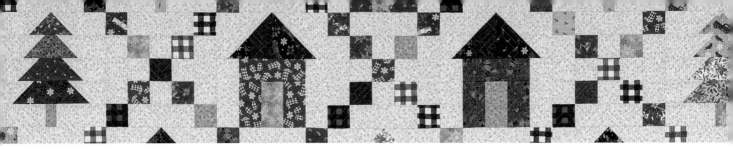

Assembling the Quilt Top

1. Lay out the blocks in seven rows of seven blocks each as shown in the quilt assembly diagram below. Sew the blocks into rows. Join the rows to make the quilt center. The quilt center should be 70½" square, including seam allowances.

2. Sew together the black print 2½" × 42" strips end to end to make one long strip. Cut the strip into two 70½"-long side border strips and two 74½"-long top and bottom border strips.

3. Sew the side border strips to the sides of the quilt center. Add the top and bottom border strips to complete the quilt top. Press all seam allowances toward the border. The finished quilt top should measure 74½" square.

Finishing the Quilt

For more details on any finishing steps, visit ShopMartingale.com/HowtoQuilt for free downloadable information.

1. Prepare the quilt backing so it's about 6" larger in both directions than the quilt top.

2. Layer the quilt top with batting and backing; baste the layers together.

3. Quilt by hand or machine. The quilt shown is machine quilted with an allover on-point square spiral design.

4. Use the red-and-black plaid 2½"-wide strips to make double-fold binding. Attach the binding to the quilt.

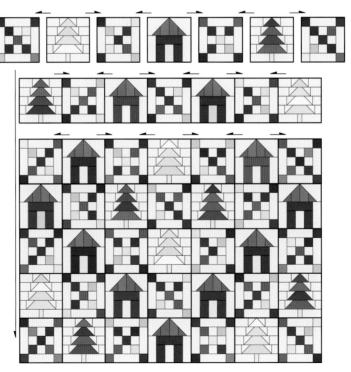

Quilt assembly

Riding the Rails

An interesting wooden fence railing was the inspiration for Michele's original block design that's easy and quick to piece together. The bright, fun prints create a quilt that is bursting with color.

Finished quilt: 69½" × 71½" ✳ Finished blocks: 19" × 14"

Materials

Yardage is based on 42"-wide fabric and one Jelly Roll (precut 2½" strips). A Moda Fabrics Jelly Roll contains 40 strips. Michele used the Love, Lily collection by April Rosenthal for Moda Fabrics.

- 36 strips, 2½" × 42" *each*, of assorted prints for blocks
- 1⅝ yards of off-white solid for blocks
- 1⅞ yards of aqua print for sashing and border
- ⅝ yard of multicolored floral for binding
- 4¼ yards of fabric for backing
- 76" × 78" piece of batting

Cutting

All measurements include ¼"-wide seam allowances. Sort the 2½"-wide strips into 12 sets of 3 fabrics each, ensuring a nice mix of colors and prints in each block. Label the strips in each set A, B, and C. Keep the pieces for each block separate so they don't get mixed up.

From *each* of the A strips, cut:
4 pieces, 2½" × 6½" (48 total)
4 squares, 2½" × 2½" (48 total)

From *each* of the B strips, cut:
2 pieces, 2½" × 7½" (24 total)
2 pieces, 2½" × 6½" (24 total)

From *each* of the C strips, cut:
2 strips, 2½" × 12½" (24 total)

From the off-white solid, cut:
34 strips, 1½" × 42"; crosscut into:
- 24 strips, 1½" × 19½"
- 24 strips, 1½" × 13½"
- 24 strips, 1½" × 12½"
- 84 pieces, 1½" × 2½"

From the aqua print, cut:
17 strips, 3½" × 42"; crosscut 4 *of the strips* into
8 strips, 3½" × 14½"

From the multicolored floral, cut:
8 strips, 2½" × 42"

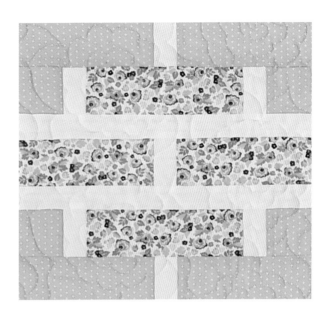

Making the Blocks

Press seam allowances in the directions indicated by the arrows. Use one A, one B, and one C fabric to make each block.

1. Sew an A 2½" × 6½" piece to each side of an off-white 1½" × 2½" piece to make unit 1. The unit should be 2½" × 13½", including seam allowances. Make 24 of unit 1 (12 pairs of matching units).

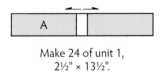

Make 24 of unit 1,
2½" × 13½".

2. Join two A 2½" squares, two off-white 1½" × 2½" pieces, and one B 2½" × 7½" piece to make unit 2. The unit should be 2½" × 13½", including seam allowances. Make 24 of unit 2 (12 pairs of matching units).

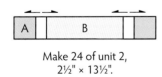

Make 24 of unit 2,
2½" × 13½".

3. Sew a B 2½" × 6½" piece to each side of an off-white 1½" × 2½" piece to make unit 3. The unit should be 2½" × 13½", including seam allowances. Make 12 of unit 3.

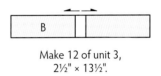

Make 12 of unit 3,
2½" × 13½".

4. Lay out two of unit 1, two of unit 2, two off-white 1½" × 13½" strips, and one of unit 3 as shown. Sew together the pieces to make the block center, which should be 13½" × 12½", including seam allowances. Make 12 block centers.

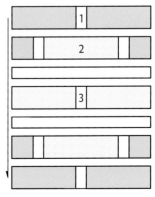

Make 12 block centers,
13½" × 12½".

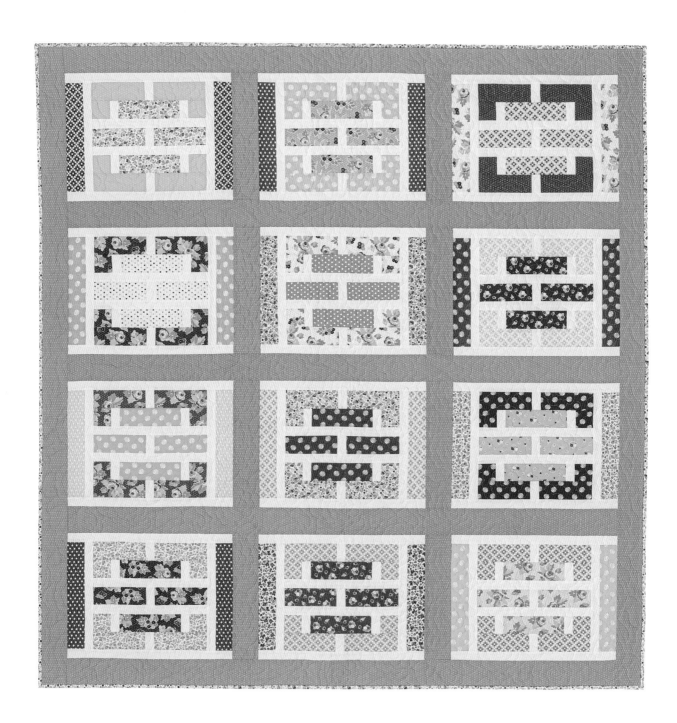

Designed and made by Michele Kuhns

See more of Michele's patterns on Instagram @crayonboxsquiltstudio.

5. Sew off-white 1½" × 12½" strips to the sides of a block center. Add C 2½" × 12½" strips to the sides. Sew off-white 1½" × 19½" strips to the top and bottom to make a block measuring 19½" × 14½", including seam allowances. Make 12 blocks.

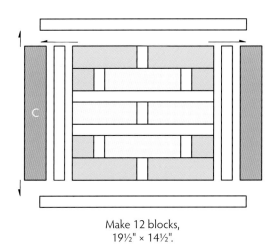

Make 12 blocks,
19½" × 14½".

Assembling the Quilt Top

1. Sew together the aqua 3½" × 42" strips end to end to make one long strip. Cut the strip into five 63½"-long horizontal sashing strips and two 71½"-long vertical sashing strips.

2. Lay out the blocks and aqua sashing strips in nine rows as shown in the quilt assembly diagram below. Sew the blocks and aqua 3½" × 14½" sashing strips into rows. Join the block rows and 63½" horizontal sashing strips. Add the 71½" vertical sashing strips to the sides to complete the quilt top, which should measure 69½" × 71½".

Finishing the Quilt

For more details on any finishing steps, visit ShopMartingale.com/HowtoQuilt for free downloadable information.

1. Prepare the quilt backing so it's about 6" larger in both directions than the quilt top.

2. Layer the quilt top with batting and backing; baste the layers together.

3. Quilt by hand or machine. The quilt shown is machine quilted with an allover flower pattern.

4. Use the multicolored floral 2½"-wide strips to make double-fold binding. Attach the binding to the quilt.

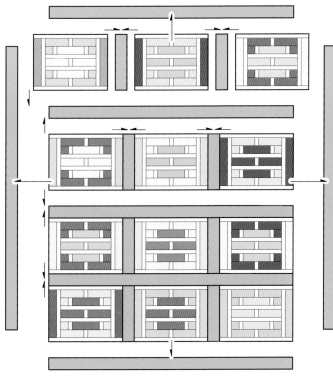

Quilt assembly

Chain Links

Easy blocks sewn with nothing but squares and rectangles create a fun design. When set together, the large "O" blocks form a secondary chain block that makes the design look like links in a lovely bracelet or necklace.

Finished quilt: 92½" × 92½" ✻ **Finished blocks: 16" × 16"**

Materials

Yardage is based on 42"-wide fabric and one Jelly Roll (precut 2½" strips). A Moda Fabrics Jelly Roll contains 40 strips. Sharla used the Spring Chicken collection by Sweetwater for Moda Fabrics. Divide your Jelly Roll into like colors as noted below.

- 6 strips, 2½" × 42" *each*, of assorted pink prints for blocks
- 6 strips, 2½" × 42" *each*, of assorted green prints for blocks
- 6 strips, 2½" × 42" *each*, of assorted yellow prints for blocks
- 6 strips, 2½" × 42" *each*, of assorted gray prints for blocks
- 3 strips, 2½" × 42" *each*, of assorted light prints for sashing squares
- 10 strips, 2½" × 42" *each*, of assorted prints for binding
- 6⅝ yards of white solid for block background and sashing
- 8½ yards of fabric for backing
- 101" × 101" piece of batting

Cutting

All measurements include ¼"-wide seam allowances.

From *each* of the pink print strips, cut:
4 pieces, 2½" × 4½" (24 total)
7 squares, 2½" × 2½" (42 total)

From the pink print scraps, cut a *total* of:
1 piece, 2½" × 4½"
8 squares, 2½" × 2½"

From *each* of the green print strips, cut:
4 pieces, 2½" × 4½" (24 total)
7 squares, 2½" × 2½" (42 total)

From the green print scraps, cut a *total* of:
1 piece, 2½" × 4½"
8 squares, 2½" × 2½"

From *each* of the yellow print strips, cut:
4 pieces, 2½" × 4½" (24 total)
7 squares, 2½" × 2½" (42 total)

From the yellow print scraps, cut a *total* of:
1 piece, 2½" × 4½"
8 squares, 2½" × 2½"

From *each* of the gray print strips, cut:
4 pieces, 2½" × 4½" (24 total)
7 squares, 2½" × 2½" (42 total)

Continued on page 44

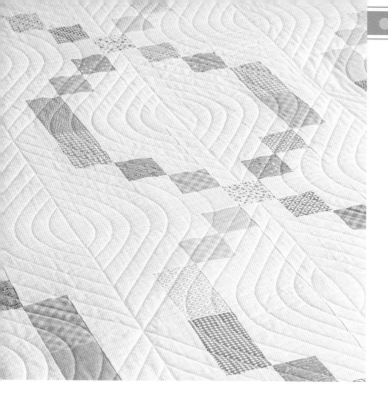

2. Repeat step 1 to make 25 each of green, yellow, and gray four-patch units.

3. Join one each of pink and yellow 2½" × 4½" pieces to make an A unit measuring 2½" × 8½", including seam allowances. Make 25 units.

Make 25 A units,
2½" × 8½".

4. Join one each of green and gray 2½" × 4½" pieces to make a B unit measuring 2½" × 8½", including seam allowances. Make 25 units.

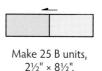

Make 25 B units,
2½" × 8½".

5. Paying attention to the orientation of the four-patch units, lay out one four-patch unit of each color, one each of units A and B, and five white 4½" × 8½" pieces in three rows. Sew together the pieces in each row. Join the rows to make a block measuring 16½" square, including seam allowances. Make 25 blocks.

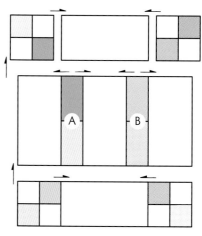

Make 25 blocks,
16½" × 16½".

Continued from page 42

From the gray print scraps, cut a *total* of:

1 piece, 2½" × 4½"

8 squares, 2½" × 2½"

From the light print strips, cut a *total* of:

36 squares, 2½" × 2½"

From the white solid, cut:

14 strips, 8½" × 42"; crosscut into 125 pieces,
   4½" × 8½"

39 strips, 2½" × 42"; crosscut into:
   • 60 strips, 2½" × 16½"
   • 200 squares, 2½" × 2½"

Making the Blocks

Press seam allowances in the directions indicated by the arrows.

1. Sew together two pink and two white 2½" squares in two rows. Join the rows to make a pink four-patch unit measuring 4½" square, including seam allowances. Make 25 units.

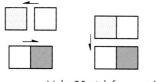

Make 25 pink four-patch units,
4½" × 4½".

Rollin' Along

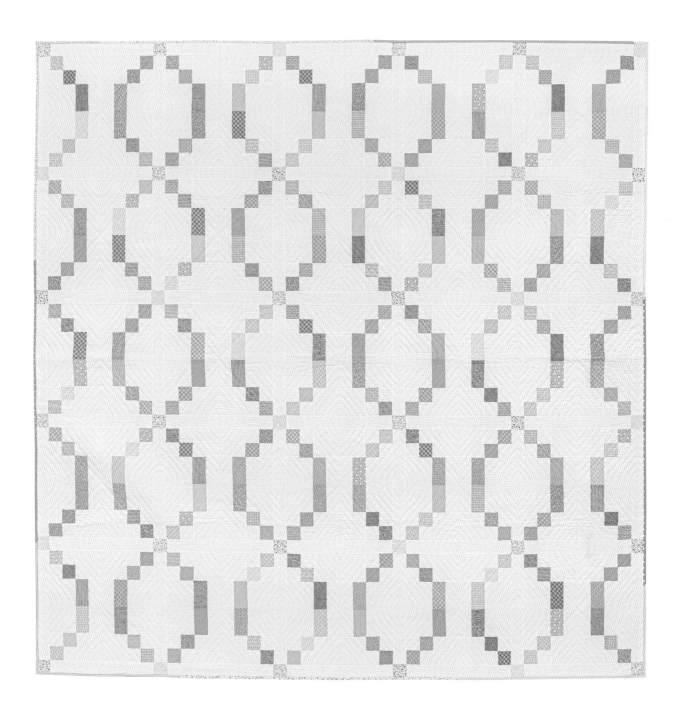

Designed and made by Sharla Krenzel

Follow Sharla on Instagram @thistlethicketstudio.

Assembling the Quilt Top

1. Join five white 2½" × 16½" strips alternating with six light print 2½" squares to make a sashing row measuring 2½" × 92½", including seam allowances. Make six rows.

Make 6 rows, 2½" × 92½".

2. Lay out five blocks alternating with six white 2½" × 16½" strips to make a row, rotating every other block 180º as shown. Join to make a block row measuring 16½" × 92½", including seam allowances. Make five rows.

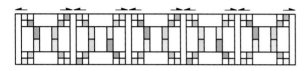

Make 5 rows, 16½" × 92½".

3. Lay out the block rows and sashing rows, alternating them as shown in the quilt assembly diagram below. Rotate the second and fourth block rows 180° as shown. Join the rows to complete the quilt top, which should measure 92½" square.

Finishing the Quilt

For more details on any finishing steps, visit ShopMartingale.com/HowtoQuilt for free downloadable information.

1. Prepare the quilt backing so it's about 8" larger in both directions than the quilt top.

2. Layer the quilt top with batting and backing; baste the layers together.

3. Quilt by hand or machine. The quilt shown is machine quilted with echoing curvy diamonds.

4. Use the assorted print 2½"-wide strips to make double-fold binding. Attach the binding to the quilt.

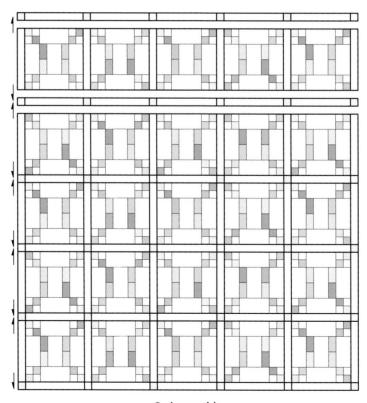

Quilt assembly

Storm Warning

You'll have nothing but smooth sailing ahead with this quilt pattern. While it may look as if set-in seams form the frames around the center squares in each block, you'll simply cut triangles from strip sets to form the framed blocks. The blocks look great in any fabrics, but stripes are particularly impressive.

Finished quilt: 56½" × 68½" ✳ **Finished blocks: 16" × 16"**

Materials

Yardage is based on 42"-wide fabric and one Jelly Roll (precut 2½" strips). A Moda Fabrics Jelly Roll contains 40 strips. Anne used the Northport collection by Minick and Simpson for Moda Fabrics.

- 36 strips, 2½" × 42" *each*, of assorted prints for blocks
- 1¾ yards of navy print for sashing and border
- ⅝ yard of multicolored stripe for binding
- 3½ yards of fabric for backing
- 63" × 75" piece of batting
- Acrylic 6½" × 6½" square ruler with diagonal marking

Cutting

All measurements include ¼"-wide seam allowances.

From the *lengthwise* grain of the navy print, cut:

2 strips, 8½" × 56½"

6 strips, 2½" × 52½"; crosscut 2 of the strips into 6 strips, 2½" × 16½"

From the multicolored stripe, cut:

7 strips, 2½" × 42"

Making the Blocks

Press seam allowances in the directions indicated by the arrows.

1. Offsetting the ends by 2½", sew together two contrasting print 2½" × 42" strips to make a strip set. Make 18 strip sets.

2½"

Make 18 strip sets, offsetting ends.

2. Align the diagonal line of the acrylic ruler with the bottom edge of a strip set. The tip of the ruler will extend just a little past the bottom of the strip set and that's OK. Cut the triangle from the strip set, then align the diagonal line with the top of the strip set to cut the second triangle. Continue until you have eight triangles (two sets of four matching triangles).

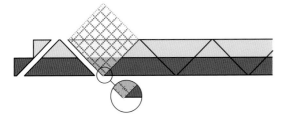

Cut 8 triangles.

3. Being careful not to stretch the bias edges, sew four matching triangles in pairs. Join the pairs to make an hourglass unit. Repeat with the remaining four triangles to make a contrasting hourglass unit. Each unit should be 8½" square, including seam allowances.

Make 2 contrasting units,
8½" × 8½".

4. Repeat steps 2 and 3 to make a total of 36 hourglass units.

5. Sew together four hourglass units in two rows of two units. Join the rows to make a block measuring 16½" square, including seam allowances. Make nine blocks.

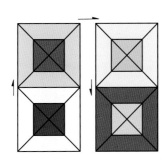

Make 9 blocks,
16½" × 16½".

Storm Warning

Designed and pieced by Anne Wiens; quilted by Doris Koontz
using Anchors Away design by Karlee Porter

See more from Anne at SweetgrassDesigns.wordpress.com.

Rollin' Along

Assembling the Quilt Top

Lay out the blocks, navy 2½" × 16½" sashing strips, and navy 2½" × 52½" sashing strips in seven columns as shown in the quilt assembly diagram below. Sew the blocks and sashing strips into rows. Join the rows. Sew the navy 8½" × 56½" border strips to the top and bottom edges to complete the quilt top, which should measure 56½" × 68½".

Finishing the Quilt

For more details on any finishing steps, visit ShopMartingale.com/HowtoQuilt for free downloadable information.

1. Prepare the quilt backing so it's about 6" larger in both directions than the quilt top.

2. Layer the quilt top with batting and backing; baste the layers together.

3. Quilt by hand or machine. The quilt shown is machine quilted with an allover anchor design.

4. Use the striped 2½" × 42" strips to make double-fold binding. Attach the binding to the quilt.

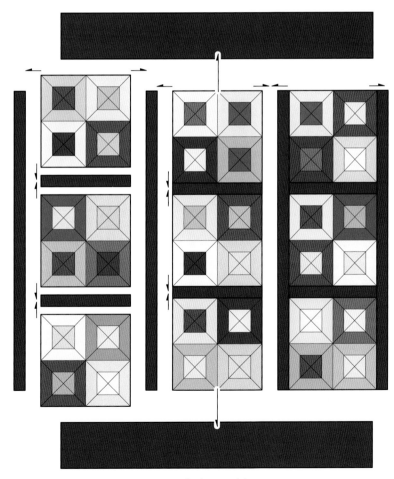

Quilt assembly

Hummingbirds

Jelly Rolls and traditional Dresden Plate blocks are a swirly-whirly
match made in heaven, especially when they're pieced into bright
flower petals and brilliant hummingbird wings!

Finished quilt: 54½" × 54½" * Finished blocks: 12" × 12"

Materials

Yardage is based on 42"-wide fabric and one Jelly
Roll (precut 2½" strips). Fat quarters measure
18" × 21". A Moda Fabrics Jelly Roll contains 40
strips. Nicola used the Stay Gold collection by
Melody Miller for Ruby Star Society.

- 37 strips, 2½" × 42" *each*, of assorted prints
  for blocks
- 1 fat quarter of teal print for flower centers and
  bird beaks and wings
- 3 yards of white solid for block backgrounds
  and border
- ½ yard of teal print for binding
- 3½ yards of fabric for backing
- 61" × 61" piece of batting
- Template plastic
- Pencil or water-soluble marking pen
- Acrylic 6" × 6" square (or larger) ruler

Cutting

All measurements include ¼"-wide seam
allowances. Before cutting, choose five assorted
strips for the hummingbird bodies. Trace the large
and small circle patterns and wedge pattern on
page 61 onto template plastic and cut out the
shapes on the drawn lines. Trace the large circle
template onto the wrong side of the teal print as
indicated below. Save the small circle and wedge
plastic templates for preparing the shapes.

From *each of 5* assorted print strips, cut:
5 pieces, 2½" × 5½" (25 total)
2 pieces, 2½" × 4½" (10 total)

From *each of the 32* remaining print strips, cut:
7 pieces, 2½" × 5½" (224 total; 4 will be extra)

From the assorted print scraps, cut a *total* of:
5 pieces, 1½" × 2½" (for hummingbird heads)

Continued on page 54

Continued from page 52

From the teal print, refer to the diagram below to cut:

11 large circles

5 pieces, 1½" × 3"

5 squares, 2½" × 2½"

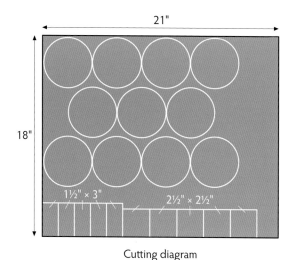

Cutting diagram

From the white solid, cut:

4 strips, 12½" × 42"; crosscut into 11 squares, 12½" × 12½"

1 strip, 7½" × 42"; crosscut into 5 squares, 7½" × 7½"

1 strip, 4½" × 42"; crosscut into 5 pieces, 4½" × 5½"

9 strips, 3½" × 42"; crosscut *3 of the strips* into:
- 5 strips, 3½" × 12½"
- 5 pieces, 3½" × 5½"
- 5 pieces, 2½" × 3½"

1 strip, 2½" × 42"; crosscut into 10 squares, 2½" × 2½"

1 strip, 1½" × 42"; crosscut into 5 squares, 1½" × 1½"

From the teal solid, cut:

6 strips, 2½" × 42"

Making the Quarter Units

Press seam allowances in the directions indicated by the arrows.

1. Fold a print 2½" × 5½" piece in half lengthwise, right sides together. Sew across one short end using a ¼" seam allowance. Clip into the corner to reduce bulk, then turn right sides out, using a knitting needle (or something similar) to form a crisp point. Line up the seam with the centerline and press. Make 245 wedge units total.

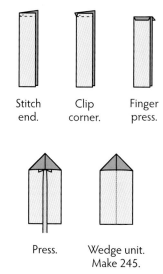

2. Slip the prepared wedge template into the wrong side of a wedge unit, matching the pointed tops. Mark the stitching lines as shown along the long edges of the template.

Mark sewing lines on wedge units.

3. Place two wedge units right sides together, making sure the stitching lines match at the pointed end (the seam is marked with a blue dot on the diagram) and pin. To ensure that the wedge won't pull apart, start ¼" from the dot and backstitch a few stitches before sewing along the stitching line. Trim the excess fabric ¼" from the seam. Carefully clip the threads and press to one side.

4. Add three more wedge units in the same manner to make a quarter unit. Press. Repeat to make 49 quarter units, being sure to press all seam allowances in the same direction.

Make 49 quarter units.

5. In each quarter unit, the two remaining stitching lines (shown in blue on the diagram) should be at right angles. Position the acrylic ruler on a quarter unit with the ruler's edges ¼" beyond the marked stitching lines. Trim the excess. If the stitching lines are not quite at right angles, use the right-angle corner of the ruler to square up the unit, making sure that it is ¼" from the points marked with a dot.

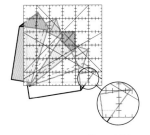 

Trim ¼" from marked stitching lines using square ruler to ensure 90° angle.

Designed and pieced by Nicola Dodd; quilted by Jayne Brereton.

Visit Nicola at CakeStandQuilts.com.

Making the Flower Blocks

1. Sew together four trimmed quarter units in two rows of two. Press seam allowances in same direction as they are pressed in the wedge units. Make 11 flower units. (You will use the remaining quarter units to make the Hummingbird blocks.)

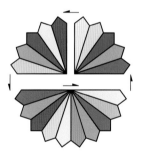

Make 11 flower units.

2. Fold a white 12½" square in half horizontally and vertically and finger-press the folds to make placement lines. Center a flower unit on the white square and pin it in place. Topstitch by machine close to the outside edge or hand appliqué in place to make a Flower block measuring 12½" square, including seam allowances. Make 11 blocks.

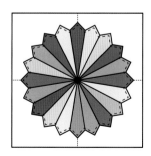

Make 11 blocks,
12½" × 12½".

3. Hand sew a running stitch around a large teal circle, about ⅛" from the edge. Place the small circle template on the wrong side of the stitched circle and pull the threads to gather the fabric over the template. Press gently and then allow to cool before removing the template. Prepare 11 teal circles in the same manner.

Prepare 11 teal circles.

4. Pin a prepared teal circle in the center of each Flower block. Topstitch by machine close to the outside edge or hand appliqué in place.

Sew teal circles to Flower blocks.

Making the Hummingbird Blocks

1. Align a trimmed quarter unit with one corner of a white 7½" square; pin in place. Topstitch by machine close to the pointed edges or hand appliqué in place to make a wing unit measuring 7½" square, including seam allowances. (You do not need to appliqué the long edges along the block corner.) Keep the pins in place for the next step. Make five units.

Make 5 wing units,
7½" × 7½".

5. Sew together a 2½" × 4½" piece and a 1½" × 2½" piece from contrasting prints. Position a marked white 1½" square in the upper-left corner of the joined pieces and a marked white 2½" square on the bottom end. Sew on the marked lines. Trim the fabric ¼" from the seam to make a body unit measuring 2½" × 5½", including seam allowances. Make three units.

Make 3 units,
2½" × 5½".

6. Trim a teal 1½" × 3" piece at an angle, starting in the upper-left corner and ending at a point ¾" from the left corner on the bottom edge to make a beak piece. Discard the smaller portion. Make three beak pieces.

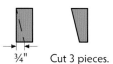

¾"   Cut 3 pieces.

2. Mark a diagonal line on the wrong side of each teal 2½" square. Align a marked square in the corner of a wing unit, right sides together. Sew on the marked line. Trim the excess fabric ¼" from the seam. Repeat with the remaining wing units.

Make 5 units,
7½" × 7½".

3. Draw a line from corner to corner on the wrong side of the white 2½" and 1½" squares.

4. Position a marked white 2½" square on one end of a print 2½" × 4½" piece. Sew on the marked line. Trim the excess fabric ¼" from the seam to make a tail unit measuring 2½" × 4½", including seam allowances. Make three units.

7. Mark a placement line that slants from ½" down from the top to 2" in from left edge on a white 3½" × 5½" piece. Position a beak piece, right sides together, on the placement line. Sew using a ¼" seam allowance. Flip the beak piece open and press. From the wrong side, trim the excess beak piece even with the edges of the white piece to make a beak unit. Make three units.

2"
½"

Make 3 units,
3½" × 5½".

Make 3 units,
2½" × 4½".

Rollin' Along

8. Sew a tail unit to a white 2½" × 3½" piece, then add a wing unit to the top of the joined pieces. Sew together a body unit and a beak unit; add a white 4½" × 5½" piece to the top of the joined edges. Join the two portions of the block together, then add a white 3½" × 12½" strip to the bottom edge of the joined sections to make a Hummingbird block measuring 12½" square. Make three blocks.

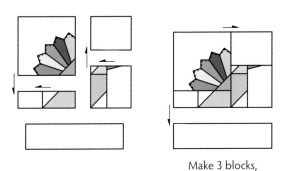

Make 3 blocks,
12½" × 12½".

9. Reversing placement of pieces, repeat steps 4–7 to make two mirror-images each of the tail, body, and beak units. Repeat step 8 to make two mirror-image blocks.

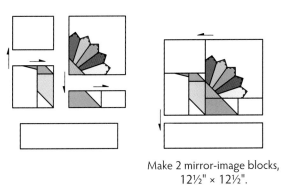

Make 2 mirror-image blocks,
12½" × 12½".

Mirror, Mirror

Turn a completed Hummingbird block to the wrong side to use as a guide when making the mirror-image blocks.

Assembling the Quilt Top

1. Lay out the blocks in four rows of four blocks each as shown in the quilt assembly diagram. Sew the blocks into rows. Join the rows to make the quilt center, which should measure 48½" square, including seam allowances.

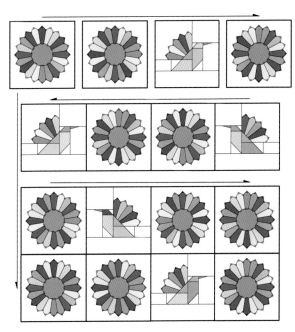

Quilt assembly

2. Referring to the adding borders diagram on page 60, sew together the remaining white 3½" × 42" strips end to end to make one long strip. Cut the strip into two 48½"-long side border strips and two 54½"-long top/bottom border strips.

3. Sew the side border strips to the sides of the quilt center. Add the top/bottom border strips to the top and bottom edges to complete the quilt top. The quilt top should measure 54½" square.

Finishing the Quilt

For more details on any finishing steps, visit ShopMartingale.com/HowtoQuilt for free downloadable information.

1. Prepare the quilt backing so it's about 6" larger in both directions than the quilt top.

2. Layer the quilt top with batting and backing; baste the layers together.

3. Quilt by hand or machine. The quilt shown is machine quilted with an allover swirly leaf and flower design.

4. Use the teal print 2½"-wide strips to make double-fold binding. Attach the binding to the quilt.

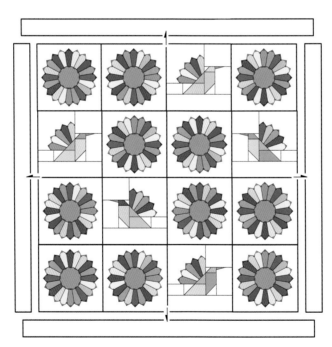

Adding borders

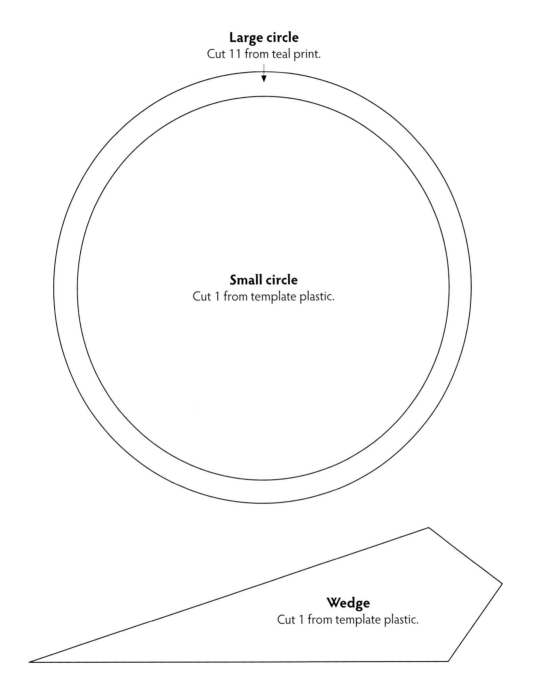

Large circle
Cut 11 from teal print.

Small circle
Cut 1 from template plastic.

Wedge
Cut 1 from template plastic.

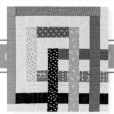

Crossroads

All of us find ourselves at a crossroad at various times. It may be a physical one as we're on a road trip, having a good time. However, many crossroads are ponderable life choices. Do we change jobs? Stay in a difficult relationship? Move to a new city? For many, the most important choice is: do we choose to find the joy and positivity in life? In Crossroads, the fabric layout is completely random, kind of like life. Lisa Jo cut and made one block at a time to keep the flow of broken lines organized.

Finished quilt: 80½" × 80½" ✳ Finished blocks: 20" × 20"

Materials

Yardage is based on 42"-wide fabric and two Jelly Rolls (precut 2½" strips). A Moda Fabrics Jelly Roll contains 40 strips. Lisa Jo used the Heirloom and First Light collections by Alexia Abegg for Ruby Star Society.

- 71 strips, 2½" × 42" *each*, of assorted prints for blocks
- 2⅞ yards of white solid for block backgrounds
- 9 strips, 2½" × 42" *each*, of assorted prints for binding
- 7½ yards of fabric for backing
- 89" × 89" piece of batting

Cutting

All measurements include ¼"-wide seam allowances.

From the white solid, cut:

42 strips, 2½" × 42"; crosscut into:

- 16 strips, 2½" × 14½"
- 64 pieces, 2½" × 6½"
- 16 pieces, 2½" × 4½" "
- 288 squares, 2½" × 2½"

Cutting and Making the Blocks

Press seam allowances in the directions indicated by the arrows. (Or press all seam allowances open.) From the 71 assorted print strips, select 10 prints for each block and label them A–J (you will use the remainder of the strip in other blocks as desired). Refer to the block diagram below to see where each print is used in the block.

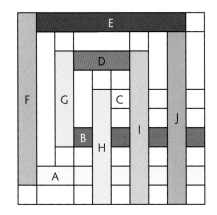

Crossroads block

From strip A, cut:

1 piece, 2½" × 4½"

4 squares, 2½" × 2½"

Continued on page 64

Continued from page 62

From strip B, cut:

4 squares, 2½" × 2½"

From strip C, cut:

3 squares, 2½" × 2½"

From strip D, cut:

1 piece, 2½" × 6½"

From strip E, cut:

1 strip, 2½" × 16½"

From strip F, cut:

1 strip, 2½" × 18½"

From strip G, cut:

1 strip, 2½" × 10½"

From strip H, cut:

1 strip, 2½" × 12½"

From strip I, cut:

1 strip, 2½" × 16½"

From strip J, cut:

1 strip, 2½" × 18½"

1. Sew white squares to the top and bottom of the print G strip. The unit should be 2½" × 14½", including seam allowances.

Make 1 unit,
2½" × 14½".

2. Sew a white 2½" × 14½" strip to the left edge of the step 1 unit. Add 2½" × 4½" white and A pieces to the bottom of the unit. The unit should be 4½" × 18½", including seam allowances.

Make 1 unit,
4½" × 18½".

3. Lay out one white 2½" × 6½" piece, seven white squares, two A squares, two B squares, one C square, and the H strip in three columns as shown. Sew together the pieces in each column. Each column should be 2½" × 14½", including seam allowances.

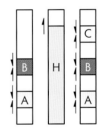

Make 3 columns, 2½" × 14½".

4. Join the columns from step 3. Add 2½" × 6½" white and D pieces to the top of the joined strips. The unit should be 6½" × 18½", including seam allowances.

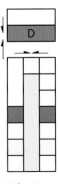

Make 1 unit,
6½" × 18½".

Designed, pieced, and quilted by Lisa Jo Girodat

Visit Lisa Jo on Instagram @neverlandstitches.

5. Lay out the seven white squares, the I strip, two white 2½" × 6½" pieces, two A squares, two B squares, and two C squares in three columns as shown. Sew together the pieces in each column. Each column should be 2½" × 18½", including seam allowances.

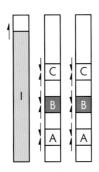

Make 3 columns,
each 2½" × 18½".

6. Join the J strip and the columns from step 5. The unit should be 8½" × 18½", including seam allowances.

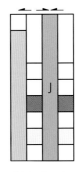

Make 1 unit,
8½" × 18½".

7. Sew together the units from steps 2, 4, and 6. The unit should be 18½" square, including seam allowances.

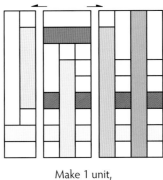

Make 1 unit,
18½" × 18½".

8. Join the E strip and a white square. Sew this unit to the top of the unit from step 7. The unit should be 20½" × 18½", including seam allowances.

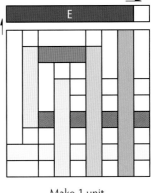

Make 1 unit,
18½" × 20½".

Rollin' Along

9. Sew together a white square and the F strip. Sew this unit to the left edge of the unit from step 8 to make a Crossroads block. The block should be 20½" square, including seam allowances.

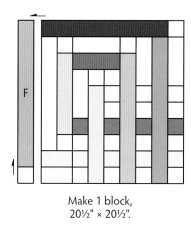

Make 1 block,
20½" × 20½".

10. Repeat to make 16 blocks, mixing up the color and print placement in each block.

Assembling the Quilt Top

Lay out the blocks in four rows of four blocks each as shown in the quilt assembly diagram below. Sew the blocks into rows. Join the rows to complete the quilt top, which should measure 80½" square.

Finishing the Quilt

For more details on any finishing steps, visit ShopMartingale.com/HowtoQuilt for free downloadable information.

1. Prepare the quilt backing so it's about 8" larger in both directions than the quilt top.

2. Layer the quilt top with batting and backing; baste the layers together.

3. Quilt by hand or machine. The quilt shown is machine quilted with an allover design of square and rectangular spirals.

4. Use the assorted print 2½"-wide strips to make double-fold binding. Attach the binding to the quilt.

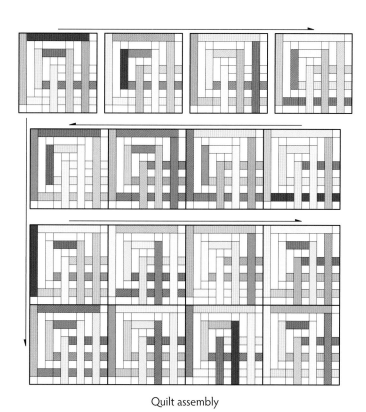

Quilt assembly

Family Reunion

Different-sized Granny Square blocks come together in this quilt for a rollicking family reunion! Join the fun by using Jelly Roll strips to make medallion-style rounds all the way from great-granny to baby-sized blocks.

Finished quilt: 62½" × 62½"
Finished blocks: 17", 8½", 5⅝", and 2⅞" square

Materials

Yardage is based on 42"-wide fabric and one Jelly Roll (precut 2½" strips). A Moda Fabrics Jelly Roll contains 40 strips. Christine used the Cozy Up Collection by Corey Yoder of Coriander Quilts for Moda Fabrics. Divide your Jelly Roll into like colors as noted below.

- 8 strips, 2½" × 42" *each*, of assorted light prints for blocks (2 matching strips and 6 additional strips)
- 3 strips, 2½" × 42" *each*, of assorted green prints for blocks
- 2 strips, 2½" × 42" *each*, of assorted gold prints for blocks
- 7 strips, 2½" × 42" *each*, of assorted aqua prints for blocks
- 7 strips, 2½" × 42" *each*, of assorted orange prints for blocks
- 5 strips, 2½" × 42" *each*, of assorted dark gray prints for blocks
- 3⅞ yards of white solid for blocks, sashing, and border
- ⅝ yard of orange floral for binding
- 3⅞ yards of fabric for backing
- 69" × 69" piece of batting

Cutting

All measurements include ¼"-wide seam allowances. You will cut the fabrics for the blocks in the following section.

From the white solid, cut:

1 strip, 6⅛" × 42"; crosscut into 28 pieces, 1¼" × 6⅛"

7 strips, 4½" × 42"; crosscut into 57 squares, 4½" × 4½". Cut the squares into quarters diagonally to yield 228 large triangles.

2 strips, 3⅜" × 42"; crosscut into 68 pieces, ⅞" × 3⅜"

15 strips, 2¾" × 42"; crosscut into 218 squares, 2¾" × 2¾". Cut the squares in half diagonally to yield 436 small triangles.

6 strips, 2½" × 42"

2 strips, 2" × 42"; crosscut into:
- 2 strips, 2" × 20½"
- 2 strips, 2" × 17½"

13 strips, 1½" × 42"; crosscut 7 *of the strips* into:
- 2 strips, 1½" × 39½"
- 2 strips, 1½" × 37½"
- 12 pieces, 1½" × 9"

From the orange floral, cut:

7 strips, 2½" × 42"

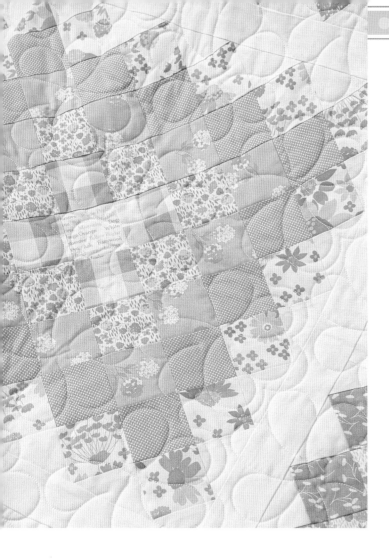

Block Assembly

Press seam allowances in the directions indicated by the arrows. Referring to the diagram, lay out the just-cut print squares in 11 diagonal rows. Place a large white triangle at each end of the rows (except row F) as shown. Sew together the pieces in each row. Join the rows. Add a small white triangle to each corner to make a Great-Granny Square block. Trim the block to 17½" square, including seam allowances.

Great-Granny Square Block

Cutting

All measurements include ¼"-wide seam allowances.

From the 2 matching light print strips, cut a *total* of:

20 squares, 2½" × 2½" (A)

From 1 green print strip, cut:

16 squares, 2½" × 2½" (B)

From 1 gold print strip, cut:

12 squares, 2½" × 2½" (C)

From 1 light print strip, cut:

8 squares, 2½" × 2½" (D)

From 1 aqua print strip, cut:

4 squares, 2½" × 2½" (E)

From 1 light print strip, cut:

1 square, 2½" × 2½" (F)

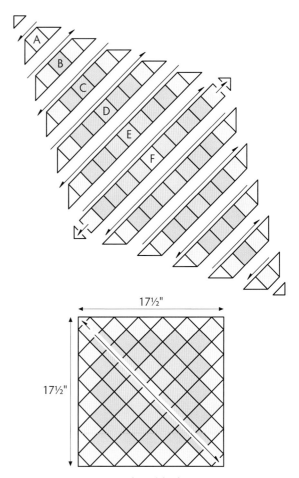

17½"

17½"

Make 1 block.

Designed and pieced by Christine Weld; quilted by Lisa Jo Girodat

Follow Christine on Instagram @christine.weld.

Granny Square Blocks

Cutting

All measurements include ¼"-wide seam allowances.

From *each of the* 6 remaining aqua print strips, cut:

16 squares, 2½" × 2½" (96 total)

From *each of the* 4 remaining light print strips, cut:

12 squares, 2½" × 2½" (48 total)

From the remaining gold print strip, cut:

12 squares, 2½" × 2½"

Block Assembly

Referring to the diagram, lay out eight matching aqua squares, four matching light squares, one gold square, and eight large white triangles in five diagonal rows. Sew together the pieces in each row. Join the rows. Add a small white triangle to each corner to make a Granny Square block. Trim the block to 9" square, including seam allowances. Make 12 blocks total.

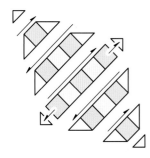
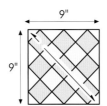

Make 12 blocks.

Perfect Placement

When sewing small triangles to the squares, fold the triangles in half and crease to mark the midpoint of the long edges. Then match the crease to the center of the square you're sewing it to.

Mama Square Blocks

Cutting

All measurements include ¼"-wide seam allowances.

From *each* of the 7 orange print strips, cut:

16 squares, 2½" × 2½" (112 total)

From *each* of the 2 remaining green print strips, cut:

14 squares, 2½" × 2½" (28 total)

Scrappy Option

If your Jelly Roll doesn't allow for seven strips of one color family, this round is a great place to go scrappy.

Block Assembly

Lay out four matching orange squares, one green square, and four large white triangles in three diagonal rows. Join the pieces in each row, then Join the rows. Add a small white triangle to each corner to make a Mama Square block. Trim the block to 6⅛" square. Make 28 blocks total.

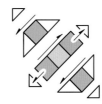

Make 28 blocks.

Baby Square Blocks

All measurements include ¼"-wide seam allowances.

Cutting

From *each* of the 5 dark gray print strips, cut:

14 squares, 2½" × 2½" (70 total; 2 are extra)

Block Assembly

Sew small white triangles to opposite edges of a gray 2½" square. Add small white triangles to the remaining edges to make a Baby Square block. Trim the block to 3⅜" square, including seam allowances. Make 68 blocks total.

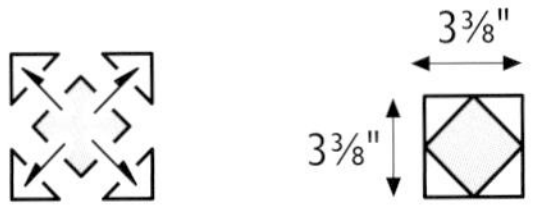

Make 68 blocks.

Assembling the Border Strips

1. Sew together three white 1½" × 9" sashing pieces and two Granny Square blocks to make a short row measuring 9" × 20½", including seam allowances. Make two rows.

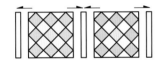

Make 2 rows, 9" × 20½".

2. Join four Granny Square blocks and three white 1½" × 9" sashing pieces to make a long row measuring 9" × 37½", including seam allowances. Make two rows.

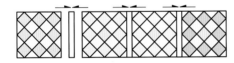

Make 2 rows, 9" × 37½".

3. Sew together seven white 1¼" × 6⅛" sashing pieces and six Mama Square blocks to make a short row measuring 6⅛" × 39½", including seam allowances. Make two rows.

Make 2 rows, 6⅛" × 39½".

4. Join eight Mama Square blocks and seven white 1¼" × 6⅛" sashing pieces to make a long row measuring 6⅛" × 50¾", including seam allowances. Make two rows.

Make 2 rows, 6⅛" × 50¾".

5. Sew together 17 white ⅞" × 3⅜" sashing pieces and 16 Baby Square blocks to make a short row. Measure the length of your strip; if necessary, trim to 52¾". Make two rows.

Make 2 rows, 3⅜" × 52¾".

6. Join 18 Baby Square blocks and 17 white ⅞" × 3⅜" sashing pieces to make a long row. Measure the length of your strip; if necessary, trim to 58½". Make two rows.

Make 2 rows, 3⅜" × 58½".

Assembling the Quilt Top

Refer to the quilt assembly diagram on page 74.

1. Sew white 2" × 17½" strips to the top and bottom edges of the Great-Granny Square block. Sew white 2" × 20½" strips to the sides. The quilt center should be 20½" square, including seam allowances.

2. Sew the short Granny Square rows to the sides of the quilt center. Sew the long Granny Square rows to the top and bottom edges. The quilt center should now be 37½" square, including seam allowances.

3. Sew white 1½" × 37½" strips to the top and bottom edges of the quilt center. Sew white 1½" × 39½" strips to the sides.

4. Sew the short Mama Square rows to the sides of the quilt center. Sew the long Mama Square rows to the top and bottom edges. The quilt center should now be 50¾" square, including seam allowances.

5. Join the six remaining white 1½" × 42" strips end to end to make one long strip. Cut the strip into two 50¾"-long border strips and two 52¾"-long border strips. Sew the 50¾"-long strips to the top and bottom and the 52¾"-long strips to the sides.

6. Sew the short Baby Square rows to the sides of the quilt center. Sew the long Baby Square rows to the top and bottom edges. The quilt center should now be 58½" square, including seam allowances.

7. Join the six white 2½" × 42" strips end to end to make one long strip. Cut the strip into two 58½"-long border strips and two 62½"-long border strips. Sew the 58½"-long strips to the sides and the 62½"-long strips to the top and bottom to complete the quilt top, which should be 62½" square.

Finishing the Quilt

For more details on any finishing steps, visit ShopMartingale.com/HowtoQuilt for free downloadable information.

1. Prepare the quilt backing so it's about 6" larger in both directions than the quilt top.

2. Layer the quilt top with batting and backing; baste the layers together.

3. Quilt by hand or machine. The quilt shown is machine quilted with an allover large flower design.

4. Use the orange floral 2½"-wide strips to make double-fold binding. Attach the binding to the quilt.

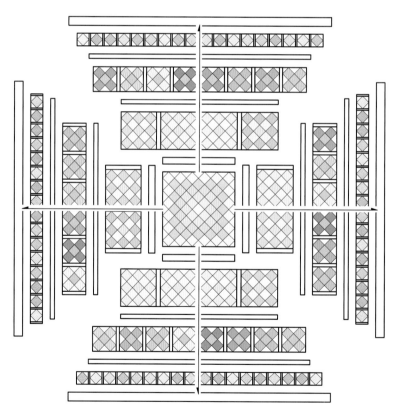

Quilt assembly

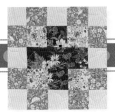

Tartan Chic

Bursts of floral patterns appear and reappear against a cream background, evoking the essence of a tartan weave. Modern colors elevate the design to a chic handmade work of art. Use two Jelly Rolls from the same line for woven perfection.

Finished quilt: 54½" × 64½" ✳ Finished blocks: 10" × 10"

Materials

Yardage is based on 42"-wide fabric and two Jelly Rolls (precut 2½" strips). A Moda Fabrics Jelly Roll contains 40 strips. Audrey and Diane used the Lady Bird collection by Crystal Manning for Moda Fabrics. Divide your Jelly Rolls into like colors as noted below.

- 10 strips, 2½" × 42" *each*, of assorted turquoise prints for Block A (2 strips *each* of 5 prints)

- 10 strips, 2½" × 42" *each*, of assorted light prints for Blocks A and B (2 strips *each* of 5 prints)

- 5 strips, 2½" × 42" *each*, of assorted navy prints for Block A

- 4 strips, 2½" × 42" *each*, of assorted aqua prints for Block B (2 strips *each* of 2 prints)

- 5 strips, 2½" × 42" *each*, of assorted orange prints for Block B

- 5 strips, 2½" × 42" *each*, of assorted yellow prints for Block B

- 6 strips, 2½" × 42" *each*, of assorted peach prints for Block B (2 strips *each* of 3 prints)

- 7 strips, 2½" × 42" *each*, of assorted green and blue prints for border

- 1⅞ yards of cream solid for background

- 7 strips, 2½" × 42" *each*, of assorted blue prints for binding

- 3½ yards of fabric for backing

- 61" × 71" piece of batting

Cutting

All measurements include ¼"-wide seam allowances.

From *each of the 5* different light prints, cut:
18 squares, 2½" × 2½" (90 total)

From *each* of the navy print strips, cut:
3 pieces, 2½" × 6½" (15 total)
6 squares, 2½" × 2½" (30 total)

From *each of the 2* different aqua prints, cut:
18 squares, 2½" × 2½" (36 total)

From *each* of the orange print strips, cut:
15 squares, 2½" × 2½" (75 total)

From *each* of the yellow print strips, cut:
12 squares, 2½" × 2½" (60 total)

From *each of the 3* different peach prints, cut:
18 squares, 2½" × 2½" (54 total)

From the assorted green and blue border strips, cut a *total* of:
57 squares, 2½" × 2½"

From the cream solid, cut:
24 strips, 2½" × 42"; crosscut *19 of the strips* into 297 squares, 2½" × 2½"

Making the A Blocks

Press seam allowances in the directions indicated by the arrows.

1. Join one cream and two matching aqua 2½" × 42" strips along the long edges, alternating colors, to make strip set A. Make five strip sets measuring 6½" × 42", including seam allowances. Cut each strip set into 12 segments, 2½" × 6½" (60 segments total).

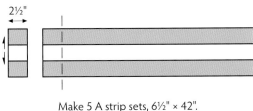

2½"

Make 5 A strip sets, 6½" × 42".
Cut 60 A segments, 2½" × 6½".
(12 from each strip set).

2. Sew matching light 2½" squares to opposite edges of a navy 2½" square. Make six matching units measuring 2½" × 6½", including seam allowances.

Make 6 units,
2½" × 6½".

3. Sew step 2 units to the long edges of a matching navy 2½" × 6½" piece to make a plus unit measuring 6½" square, including seam allowances. Make three units.

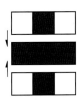

Make 3 units,
6½" × 6½".

4. Repeat steps 2 and 3 with the remaining light print and navy print pieces to make a total of 15 plus units (three units each in five different color combinations).

5. Lay out four cream 2½" squares, four matching A segments, and one plus unit in three rows. Sew together the pieces in each row. Join the rows to make an A block measuring 10½" square, including seam allowances. Make 15 A blocks (three blocks each in five different fabric combinations).

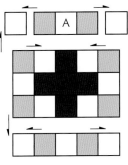

Make 15 A blocks,
10½" × 10½".

Making the B Blocks

1. Draw a diagonal line on the wrong side of 12 squares from one aqua print. Place a marked square right sides together with a cream square. Sew on the drawn line. Trim the excess fabric ¼" from the seam. The unit should still be 2½" square, including seam allowances. Repeat to make 12 half-square-triangle units from each aqua print (24 total).

Make 24 units,
2½" × 2½".

2. Arrange four matching half-square-triangle units, eight cream squares, five matching orange squares, four matching yellow squares, two matching light print 2½" squares, and two aqua squares (that match the half-square-triangle units) in five rows as shown. Sew the pieces into rows, then join the rows to make an aqua B block measuring 10½" square, including seam allowances. Make six aqua B blocks (three blocks each in two different fabric combinations).

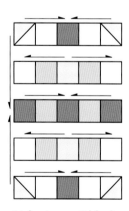

Make 6 aqua B blocks,
10½" × 10½".

3. In the same manner as step 1, make 12 half-square-triangle units from each peach print (36 total).

4. Using peach print instead of aqua print, refer to step 2 to make nine peach B blocks (three blocks each in three different fabric combinations).

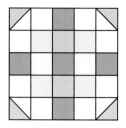

Make 9 peach B blocks,
10½" × 10½".

Assembling the Quilt Top

1. Lay out the blocks in six rows of five blocks each as shown in the quilt assembly diagram on page 80, alternating between blocks A and B and paying attention to the placement of aqua and peach B blocks. Sew the blocks into rows. Join the rows to make the quilt center, which should be 50½" × 60½", including seam allowances.

2. Alternating colors, sew together 15 green or blue and 15 cream 2½" squares to make a side border strip measuring 2½" × 60½", including seam allowances. Make two. Join 14 cream and 13 green or blue 2½" squares to make the top border strip measuring 2½" × 54½", including seam allowances. Then sew together 14 green or blue and 13 cream 2½" squares to make the bottom border strip measuring 2½" × 54½", including seam allowances.

Make 2 side strips, 2½" × 60½".

Make 1 top strip, 2½" × 54½".

Make 1 bottom strip, 2½" × 54½".

Designed and made by Audrey Mann and Diane Brinton

Follow Audrey and Diane on Instagram @theclothparcel.

3. Sew the side border strips to the sides of the quilt center. Add the top/bottom border strips to the top and bottom edges to complete the quilt top, which should be 54½" × 64½". Press the seam allowances toward the border.

Finishing the Quilt

For more details on any finishing steps, visit ShopMartingale.com/HowtoQuilt for free downloadable information.

1. Prepare the quilt backing so it's about 6" larger in both directions than the quilt top.

2. Layer the quilt top with batting and backing; baste the layers together.

3. Quilt by hand or machine. The quilt shown is machine quilted with an overall floral pattern.

4. Use the blue print 2½"-wide strips to make double-fold binding. Attach the binding to the quilt.

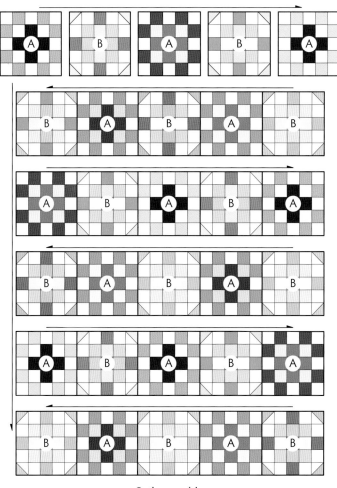

Quilt assembly